LOST LINES OF WALES
VALE OF NEATH

TOM FERRIS

GRAFFEG

CONTENTS

FOREWORD

Few parts of Britain were changed more radically in the late eighteenth and nineteenth centuries by the irresistible forces of the industrial revolution than the valleys of south Wales. Before the storm, the Valleys were thinly populated and those who lived there were largely Welsh speaking. The rise of first the iron industry and later the development of coal mining transformed the Valleys root and branch. Welsh mines produced anthracite and high-quality steam coals, which were much sought after in an age powered by steam. The population increased exponentially to meet the demands of the new industries, with many moving to the area from other parts of the United Kingdom, replacing Welsh with English as the dominant language and turning hitherto green and pleasant landscapes into wastelands scarred by the detritus of the industrial age.

To transport the coal to the ports on the Bristol Channel for export to overseas markets or to meet the insatiable demands of London and other growing cities for coal both for domestic and industrial use, a network of railways of bewildering complexity developed in the nineteenth century in and around the Valleys. This volume explores one of the most impressive and distinctive of these railways, the Vale of Neath, conceived initially to connect Merthyr and Aberdare to the port of Swansea.

However, before going any further, there are actually two definitions of what can be referred to as the Vale of Neath Railway, and different track gauges were involved from the outset. The original VoN was promoted and built as a 7ft, or, to be absolutely precise, 7ft 0 ¼ broad gauge line. This was the gauge favoured by the line's engineer, Isambard Kingdom Brunel, and the Great Western Railway, whose subsidiary, the South Wales Railway, would link the VoN to the ports of Swansea and Briton Ferry. Shortly after it opened this was joined from the east by another railway, which ran from Pontypool Road on the line between Newport and Hereford, eventually meeting the VoN at Middle Duffryn near Aberdare.

This was the Taff Vale Extension Railway, promoted by the Newport, Abergavenny & Hereford company, and was built to the standard or narrow gauge of 4ft 8½.

In time, both these railways fell into the hands of the Great Western Railway and the whole line from Neath to Pontypool Road came to be referred to as the Vale of Neath, with some passenger trains running over its entire 41 mile length. This pictorial survey will follow the Vale of Neath line as it was defined by the GWR and not the shorter route built by the original Vale of Neath company.

This is a story of two railways, one going roughly west to east and the other in the opposite direction. Built by two different companies which adopted different gauges, both were promoted to transport the abundant supplies of coal in the districts they served. We will begin this brief survey of the history of the line with the original Vale of Neath Company, the one going west to east.

The South Wales Railway was promoted in the 1840s to build a line from Gloucester down the Welsh side of the Severn Estuary to Chepstow then on to Newport, Cardiff and Swansea. From there it would head further west to a new port at Fishguard on the Pembrokeshire coast, from where steamers would sail across the Irish Sea to another new port which was to be built south of Wexford. The SWR was effectively a subsidiary of the Great Western Railway, its engineer was Isambard Kingdom Brunel and it was built to the GWR broad gauge of 7ft 0 ¼. Closely associated with the SWR was the Vale of Neath Railway, authorised by Parliament in September 1846 to build a line from Neath to run through the Glyn Neath valley to Merthyr with a branch to Aberdare. With Brunel as its engineer it was to be a broad gauge line, as the coal and other traffic it hoped to attract would be conveyed to the ports of Swansea and Briton Ferry by the SWR as it was. Initially though in 1863 the VoN opened a line of its own from Neath to Swansea, thus depriving the SWR of a share of the revenues from its coal traffic.

Construction began in 1847. The first part of the line through Glyn Neath was quite flat, but then it began to climb steeply on five miles of gradients of between 1 in 47 and 1 in 57 to reach Hirwaun. The initial plan was that the main line should go to Merthyr, but this required the building of a tunnel close to 1½ miles long. Because of the difficulties in raising money in the depressed economic conditions of the time and problems the contractors were having with the tunnel, it was decided to press on with the Aberdare line first and this opened for traffic on 24th September 1851. In June 1853, the line was extended a short distance beyond the station to the Aberdare canal basin to attract coal traffic. This did not generate much business, so in 1855 a short, but as things turned out, a very important extension was sponsored by the VoN to Middle Duffryn colliery to cut out the canal.

The VoN's two routes divided at Gelli Tawr Junction, near Hirwaun. The Merthyr line was finally opened on 2nd November 1853. Aside from the tunnel it involved more steep gradients and a long viaduct over the river at Merthyr, the existing Taff Vale Railway line to the town before it reached the VoN station at High Street, which became the terminus for all the five railway companies which eventually served Merthyr. In 1854 and 1857 respectively, two goods only lines opened from Gelli Tawr Junction, serving collieries in the Dare and Aman valleys. With the VoN system now complete, attention must shift to the east.

From the 1820s onwards, the railways began to move from the industrial fringes of Britain onto the main stage. As they became an increasingly important part of the economy, absorbing more and more capital and resources and reshaping the landscape in a way probably not seen since the time of the Romans, the new railway companies were left to get on with it by governments which did little to regulate or control their activities, until it was too late. The most glaring example of this laissez-faire attitude was that Britain's railways were being built to two different track gauges: the broad gauge of Brunel and the GWR, which was expanding across the south and west of the country, and the standard, or narrow gauge as it was often referred to in the 1830s and 40s, which was being used outside GWR territory, advocated by George and Robert Stephenson. This led to chaos at places like Gloucester, where the two gauges met with passengers and goods having to be transshipped from one to the other, and also to endless legal and parliamentary battles between the two camps in the 1840s as they jostled for territory.

As far as Wales was concerned, with the GWR's satellite the South Wales Railway extending its main line to Cardiff, Swansea and beyond, the scene was set for more gauge related chaos and conflict. One of the first significant Welsh companies, the Taff Vale Railway had begun to build its line from Cardiff to Merthyr in 1836. Ironically, its engineer, Brunel, had advised the TVR to use the narrow gauge, as this was more suitable for its sinuous route closely following the River Taff. Even that great advocate of the broad gauge realised that for railways in the steep, narrow valleys of south Wales it was not really suitable.

In 1846, the Newport, Abergavenny & Hereford Railway was promoted to link those towns. The company was supported by the London & North Western Railway, which was not only anxious to get a share of the traffic emanating from south Wales but also to forestall any expansion of the GWR and its broad gauge towards Birmingham and the midlands. The NA&H was to be a standard gauge line and would link up with the Shrewsbury & Hereford, also authorised in 1846, and a projected line from Hereford to Worcester. In 1847, the NA&H obtained another Act of Parliament for what was called the Taff Vale Extension Railway. This was a line 15½ miles long from Pontypool Road station on its main line to Hereford west to join the Taff Vale Railway at Quakers Yard near Merthyr. This would give the NA&H access to the burgeoning coal fields of the Taff, Ebbw and Aberdare Valleys.

The line began with a climb from Pontypool Road, up through the Glyn Valley on gradients as steep as 1 in 45. Rather than dipping into the Ebbw Valley to cross it, it carried on at a high level, probably to make the running of loaded eastbound coal trains as easy as possible. This meant that the line had to be taken across the valley at a height of over 200 feet on the majestic Crumlin viaduct, one of the most striking railway structures ever built in Wales. The viaduct was designed and constructed by T W Kennard, working closely with the NA&H engineer, Charles Liddell. At the time of its opening it was the third highest structure of its kind in the world, with a maximum height above the Ebbw River in the valley below of 208 feet. Built for double track at a cost of £62,000, it was 1,658 feet long, with the trackbed supported on graceful metal piers with most of the ironwork being made at a foundry set up on the site.

The line opened to the east side of the viaduct in August 1855, and across it to Pontllanfraith in June 1857. A further extension seven miles long took the TVE to Quakers Yard and a junction with the Taff Vale Railway in January 1858. The NA&H amalgamated with the West Midland Railway in 1860, which in turn was absorbed by the GWR in 1863. The GWR extended the line from Quakers Yard to a junction with the VoN at Middle Duffryn in 1864, completing the link between east and west, Pontypool Road, Neath and Swansea. The opening of this link coincided with the VoN being converted to mixed gauge, with an extra rail being added to allow through running over the erstwhile NA&H. The last part of the VoN that remained purely broad gauge was the line to Merthyr, which got a third rail too in 1867. The SWR amalgamated with the GWR in August 1863, and in February 1865 the VoN went the same way. The broad gauge in Wales did not last much longer, with all the remaining lines being converted in May 1872. This was the beginning of the end for Brunel's 7ft gauge, the last remaining lines in England being converted to standard gauge in 1892.

The Vale of Neath was seen as a through route, the relevant timetables pages usually covering the whole line from Neath to Pontypool Road, yet relatively few trains, both passenger and goods, ran over all of it. Initially, the original VoN Company had set out to build a main line from Neath to Merthyr, but the section from Gelli Tawr Junction to Merthyr, which was completed after the line to Aberdare, took on the characteristics of a branch line from the start, with connecting services to Merthyr running from Hirwaun. The line remained open for 100 years, and a couple of snapshots from twentieth century timetables show that the pattern of services that had been established in the nineteenth century did not vary greatly over the years. The summer 1922 timetable shows six trains from Neath or Swansea to Pontypool Road, and five in the other direction. In the last year of the GWR's existence, 1947, there were five through trains in each direction. All services now started or terminated at Neath General, rather than running through to Swansea, but the time allowed for the run from Neath to Pontypool Road had not improved over the years, taking about two hours for the 40 odd miles. In addition to the through trains there were a number of short workings, trains terminating at Aberdare, services running during school terms only for the benefit of scholars, and workingmen's trains, noted as such in the timetables to get miners to and from work at the many collieries along the line.

As might be expected, the Vale of Neath carried huge volumes of coal traffic throughout its existence. The South Wales coal field reached the peak of its production in 1913. In that year 56 million tons of coal was produced by a workforce of 232,800 men. Coal trains went in both directions on the Vale of Neath line, west to the docks at Swansea or Briton Ferry and eastwards to Pontypool Road, where there were large marshalling yards from whence trains were dispatched to the north and midlands or eastwards to London. Pontypool Road and Aberdare engine sheds provided most of the locomotives used on the line, which remained almost exclusively steam worked to the end of through services.

The Vale of Neath line was not one of the many routes condemned in the infamous Beeching report of 1963. This was because it was already being considered for closure before the report was published. The first closure was that of the service from Hirwaun to Merthyr, which ended on 31st December 1962, and this was followed by the withdrawal of passenger trains over the whole of the main line in June 1964. Some thought was given to preserving the magnificent Crumlin viaduct, but it was deemed to be in poor condition and was condemned. In 1966, before demolition commenced, it was the setting for some scenes in a feature film called *Arabesque,* starring Sophia Loren and Gregory Peck, that were shot on and around the viaduct. In 1967 the last parts of the ironwork were removed, leaving just the stone abutments as testament to that engineering marvel which had spanned this Welsh valley for over 100 years.

Pontypool Road was a major junction in its heyday, with acres of sidings and an engine shed that once had an allocation of over 100 locomotives. Today, all that remains is a very basic modern station on a island platform called Pontypool Road and New Inn, a pale shadow of its former self, an unstaffed halt on the line between Newport and Abergavenny at which many trains do not call. Merthyr still retains a passenger service to Cardiff via the Taff Vale Railway route to the town, and trains returned to Aberdare in 1988 using a new station built to the south of the original Vale of Neath Aberdare High Level station. The track north of Aberdare was retained for coal traffic from south Wales' last deep mine, Tower Colliery, which finally closed in 2008. Suggestions have been made that the line should be extended from Aberdare to Hirwaun, but nothing has as yet come of this.

PONTYPOOL ROAD

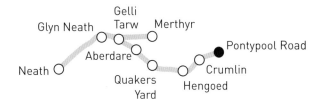

Not all of the reasonably frequent services on the line between Newport and Hereford call at Pontypool & New Inn station, which consists of a short island platform accessed by a subway. Looking at what is there today, unless you knew something of the railway history of south Wales, you would be hard pressed to realise that this was once a major junction and a busy interchange station. The two principal routes which branched off here were lines to Monmouth and

Ross-on-Wye and the one we will follow, which provided through services and connections to Aberdare, Merthyr, Neath and Swansea. In August 1936, GWR 5700 class 0-6-0 Pannier Tank No 9788 is in the south facing bay platform at Pontypool Road, used by trains on the Vale of Neath line. The locomotive at the through platform to the right is GWR Bulldog class 4-4-0 No 3308.

The station at Pontypool Road was completely rebuilt by the GWR in 1908/09. The new station consisted of a long island platform with bays at both ends. In addition, Pontypool Road had an engine shed and a great number of sidings, used to marshall and dispatch goods and coal trains to a wide range of destinations, mostly in the midlands and the north. Like today's station, the island platform was accessed through a subway under the tracks. In this view, taken from the station approach road on 15th May 1935, the locomotive on the train at the platform is Bulldog class 4-4-0 No 3372 *Sir N. Kingscote*. Saint class 4-6-0 No 2905 *Lady Macbeth* is to the right of the picture.

Pontypool Road shed was given the code 86C by BR, and in this view taken on 16th August 1954 most of the locomotives are of GWR origin, though the one blowing off steam and making all the smoke is not. This is an unidentified ex-War Department Austerity 2-8-0. Built for service during the Second World War, this is one of the 733s which entered BR service in the late 1940s. At its peak the shed had an allocation of around 100 locomotives and in 1954, even though the coal traffic which generated much of its work was in decline, there were still 90 engines based here.

Pontypool Road was somewhat to the east of the town. The station on the Taff Vale Extension line which opened in 1867 was closer. Originally this was called Pontypool Town, though from the 1880s onwards it was known as Pontypool Clarence Street. Ex-GWR 5700 class 0-6-0PT No 9607 is arriving with a train bound for Pontypool Road in this 1962 view. The line, which was double tracked, began to climb from here up through the Glyn Valley, passing Hafodyrynys colliery and through the 280 yards long Glyn Tunnel on gradients as steep as 1 in 45 in places. Goods trains going to Pontypool Road had to stop to enable the Guard to pin down the hand brakes on wagons before tackling the descent, and were restricted to 6mph on the steepest parts of the incline. The signalbox in the distance by the overbridge is Trosnant Junction on the Eastern Valley line. A spur connected the two lines here.

CRUMLIN HIGH LEVEL

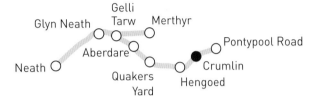

Glyn Neath

Gelli Tarw

Merthyr

Pontypool Road

Neath

Aberdare

Quakers Yard

Crumlin

Hengoed

The stiff gradients through the Glyn Valley were required in order to allow the line to cross the Ebbw Valley at Crumlin at a high level. Loaded coal trains on this part of the route, which were mostly heading for the marshalling yards at Pontypool Road, were therefore going downhill, with the lighter trains of empty wagons going in the other direction up the gradients. Having said that, as almost all mineral wagons in the steam era did not have continuous brakes, controlling a heavy train on a downward gradient with only the brakes on the engine and that of the Guard in his van at the rear was a challenge for the crews working these trains. The great viaduct at Crumlin, which took the line across the Ebbw Valley, was about six miles from Pontypool Road. On 27th September 1963, ex-GWR 0-6-2T No 6622 crosses the Crumlin viaduct with the 11.50am passenger train from Neath to Pontypool Road.

Trundling across the viaduct in the other direction is a train made up mostly of empty BR designed standard 16 ton mineral wagons, hauled by ex-GWR 0-6-0 Pannier Tank No 4639. In the 1950s, over a quarter of a million of these wagons were ordered by BR and could be seen on virtually every railway line and goods yard throughout the country, such was the dominance of 'king coal' within living memory. The viaduct had been built for double track, but was singled in the 1920s, the remaining track slewed to the centre of the decking and a speed limit of 8 mph imposed across it. Despite its great height and the seemingly slender columns which supported it, there were never any serious issues about its strength or safety throughout its working life of over 100 years.

A friend of mine who travelled over Crumlin viaduct before it closed described how the structure seemed to sigh as his train passed over it.

This was a passenger's view from a train passing over Crumlin viaduct, surely one of the most spectacular available through the window of a railway carriage anywhere in Wales. Taken on 2nd May 1959, over 200 feet below on the valley floor is Crumlin Low Level station on the Western Valleys line.

A passenger train comes off the viaduct and back onto a double track formation as it approaches Crumlin High Level station. The locomotive is ex-GWR 5600 class 0-6-2T No 6650. Before grouping, this type of wheel arrangement was popular in south Wales with the previously independent companies that became part of the GWR, the Taff Vale Railway notably operating many examples. When the GWR took over it built its own class of 0-6-2T, 200 locos being turned out between 1924 and 1928 and seen all over the former GWR lines until the end of steam operations in the 1960s. The Crumlin viaduct was actually built in two parts and consisted of two groups of three and seven 150 foot long spans, separated by a hill at the western end from where the final three spans of the structure curved round to the High Level station.

Because of the height this line attained on its climb through the Glyn Valley to cross the Ebbw Valley at Crumlin, which it retained as it headed westwards, a number of its stations, including those at Crumlin, Quakers Yard and Aberdare, were designated High Level to distinguish them from other stations serving those places on nearby lines. An exception to this was at Pontllanfraith. Here, the station on the former LNWR Sirhowy Valley line which passed over the TVE was called Pontllanfraith High Level, the former TVE station being Pontllanfraith Low Level. Ex-GWR 5700 Pannier Tank No 7724 leaves the Low Level station on 30th May 1959 with a train from Pontypool Road to Neath. Competition in the form of a Western Welsh double decker bus is also in the picture.

The main business of this line throughout its existence was the transport of coal from the many collieries located close to it. Whilst shorter workings made use of tank locomotives, the workhorse of the GWR for long distance and heavier freight trains was the 2800 class 2-8-0s. Designed by G J Churchward and introduced in 1903, these were the first 2-8-0s to run in Britain. A total of 167 were built up to 1942, later engines being modified with better driving cabs. The first of these engines to be used on the VoN were allocated to Aberdare engine shed in 1906, and between then and 1963 members of the class were always on the books of both Aberdare and Pontypool Road depots. The prototype which became No 2800 had clocked up over one and a quarter million miles when it was withdrawn in 1958. No 2876, seen here near

Hengoed in 1960, was built at Swindon in 1919 and lasted until 1965.

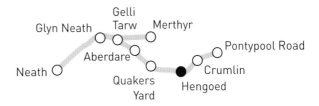

The next obstacle faced by the builders of the TVE was the crossing of the Rhymney Valley and its river. This was spanned by the Hengoed or Maesycwmmer viaduct, which carried the line on 16 stone arches, 130 feet high. At its eastern end the viaduct crossed over the line from Brecon to Merthyr (see Lost Lines of Wales, Brecon to Newport, page 57) which was connected to the TVE by a spur, opened in1863. There were also connections to the former Rhymney Railway lines on the west side of the valley. On the 7th July 1962, a goods train is seen on the viaduct approaching Hengoed High Level station.

A passenger train from Pontypool Road pauses at Hengoed High Level station in the summer of 1963. The curving western end of the viaduct can be seen behind the train to the right of the picture. The locomotive is 2-6-2 Tank No 4174. This introduces us to another of Churchward's long lived designs for the GWR, developed from a prototype built in 1903. Members of this class were built between then and 1949, which was the year when No 4174 was turned out by BR at Swindon, so while it is a GWR design it was never a GWR locomotive. As sometimes happened towards the end of steam, the locomotive's smokebox number plate has been removed and probably now still graces someone's collection of railway memorabilia.

Three miles west of Hengoed the line came to the large station of Nelson & Llancaiach, which the GWR rebuilt in 1912 a short distance to the west of the original one. This had three platforms and was the junction for the branch which ran up the Taff Bargoed valley via Bedlinog to Dowlais Cae Harris. Trains ran to Cardiff from here via Ystrad Mynach and this section of the line was also one of the busiest for coal traffic from the many collieries, spurs and sidings in the vicinity. On 18th June 1960, ex-GWR 5600 class 0-6-2T No 5625 is leaving Nelson & Llancaiach with the 11.15am train from Neath to Pontypool Road. This locomotive entered service in August 1925 and was withdrawn in October 1963. At the time of the photograph it was allocated to the engine shed at Pontypool Road.

QUAKERS YARD

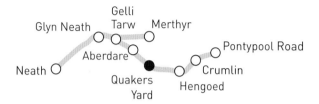

Glyn Neath · Gelli Tarw · Merthyr · Pontypool Road · Aberdare · Neath · Quakers Yard · Hengoed · Crumlin

The next major set of junctions on a line which had them in abundance was encountered at Quakers Yard, two miles beyond Nelson & Llancaiach. The place took its name from a burial ground used by the Society of Friends that was established in the eighteenth century. On 28th March 1955, a westbound goods train is seen at Quakers Yard East Junction where there was a connection to the former Taff Vale Railway route to Merthyr, the only one of the many lines to Merthyr which is still available for passengers today. The train is headed by ex-GWR 2-8-0T No 5237, another class of

heavy goods engine long associated with the Welsh Valleys. Designed by Churchward and introduced in 1910, these were the first 2-8-0Ts in Britain and shared many components with his 2800 class 2-8-0 tender engines of the same era. In the 1930s, over 50 of these locos were rebuilt as 2-8-2Ts, their greater coal and water capacity extending their range. Both types were widely used in south Wales up to the end of steam in the 1960s.

There were again High and Low Level stations here, that on the TVE being the High Level one. Ex-GWR 5600 class 0-6-2T No 6605 brings a freight train through Quakers Yard High Level station on 10th November 1956.

At the west end of the station there was another junction. The line to the left is that to Aberdare, and it became single track as it headed off towards Cefn Glas or Quakers Yard tunnel. This was the section opened by the GWR in 1864 after it had taken over the NA&H, to link the line from Pontypool Road to the original VoN at Middle Duffryn, near Aberdare. The line to the right, which opened in 1886, had been jointly owned by the GWR and the RR and ran up the west side of the Taff to Merthyr. This line's viaduct over the River Taff was affected by subsidence, leading to its closure in 1951. This view, dating from 28th March 1955 after the closure of the Joint Line, shows an engine shunting on the remains of it.

The single track through the 703 yards long Cefn Glas tunnel took the line from the Taff and into the Cynon Valley. Once clear of its narrow bore, double track was regained. There were two stations at Penrhiwceiber, the other being on the parallel Taff Vale line to Aberdare. In 1924, with both lines now under the control of the GWR, High Level and Low Level were added to their names to avoid any confusion. This is the High Level station, recorded on 27th June 1963, a modest affair with buildings and platforms of timber construction, looking towards Quakers Yard.

ABERDARE

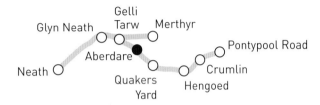

Glyn Neath · Gelli Tarw · Merthyr · Pontypool Road · Aberdare · Neath · Quakers Yard · Hengoed · Crumlin

At Aberdare we join the tracks of the original Vale of Neath line, which reached here in 1851. Aberdare High level station was on a confined site beside the River Cynon. This meant that when the line was extended to the east the platforms had to be staggered. This view looking east shows a passenger train bound for Neath leaving the westbound platform. The two platforms were connected by a covered footbridge.

In 1963, a westbound train is seen at the other platform. Ex-GWR No 6149 was a locomotive of a type which would not usually have been found in south Wales. It was part of a class of 70 2-6-2Ts built between 1931 and 1935, which spent most of their lives hauling commuter trains in and out of Paddington, the majority of the class being allocated to sheds in the GWR's London division. With these duties by now in the hands of diesels, a handful of the survivors migrated to sheds in Wales, including No 6149, which was withdrawn from Neath shed in June 1964.

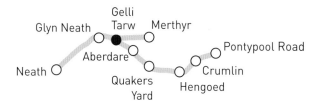

On 26th May 1954, a train hauled by ex-GWR 0-6-0 Pannier Tank No 6427 takes the branch for Merthyr at Gelli Tawr Junction. The initial intention of the promoters of the VoN was that their main line should go to Merthyr. However, delays in constructing the tunnel, which took the line through Mynydd Merthyr to reach the town, meant that the line to Aberdare opened first. The emphasis changed back to Merthyr in 1853, when the line finally opened, but reverted to Aberdare in 1864 when the connection through to

Middle Duffryn was built. From that time onwards the route to Pontypool Road was the main line, with most Merthyr trains connecting with through trains at Hirwaun. In this view, the pair of tracks in the foreground lead to Aberdare, the goods only line which served collieries in the Dare and Aman valleys is on the left.

MERTHYR

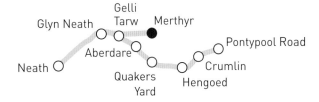

Glyn Neath · Gelli Tarw · Merthyr · Pontypool Road · Aberdare · Crumlin · Neath · Quakers Yard · Hengoed

The VoN station, close to the High Street, was the second one to open in Merthyr and was a most impressive affair, graced by the line's engineer Brunel with one of his signature overall roofs or train sheds. The Taff Vale Railway had reached the town in 1841 and already had a terminus at Plymouth Street. TVR services began to use High Street from 1877, and at the height of its pomp the station was served by the trains of five railway companies. Even after the 1923 grouping it continued to see trains from two of the 'Big Four' companies. One of those five companies had been

the LNWR, which became part of the LMS group in 1923, and services on what was known as the Heads of the Valleys line, the LNWR route from Abergavenny to Merthyr, brought LMS locomotives to High Street station. One of these is seen there on 26th April 1948, early in the BR era. Ex-LNWR Webb designed 0-6-2 Coal Tank No 27621, still in LMS livery, was one of a class of 300 locomotives built at Crewe between 1881 and 1897. This engine, dating from 1883, survived until 1955. It was renumbered 58891 by BR in 1949.

When the VoN was converted to standard gauge in 1872, this created just about enough space to squeeze in an additional island platform, albeit a very narrow one, giving High Street station a total of five platforms. On 16th July 1957, one of those workhorses of the lines in the Welsh Valleys, ex-GWR 5600 class 0-6-2T No 6638, is seen on a passenger train at the station. Today, just the original TVR line to the town remains and the station has been reduced to a single platform, the rest of the site having been redeveloped.

Hirwaun, four miles from Aberdare, was the junction for the branch to Merthyr. Passenger services on the branch ended in 1962. The GWR and BR often used Auto trains on the Merthyr line, as they did on many branch lines. This method of working avoided the need for the loco to run round its train at the terminus. When the engine was hauling the specially designed Auto trailers, the driver was on the footplate in the conventional fashion. However, going in the other direction the loco remained coupled to the rear of the set in charge of the fireman, who attended to the fire and water, whilst the driver removed himself to a driving cab in the end Auto trailer, equipped with driving and brake controls linked to the locomotive by rodding under the carriages. On 26th April 1948, Auto fitted 6400 Pannier Tank No 6427 and a pair of Auto trailers will form the 12.20pm service to Merthyr. The driving cabs of Auto trailers, such as the one next to the loco, had large windows to give a good view of the track ahead when the trailers were being propelled. Four

months into BR ownership, No 6427 still has the GWR initials on the side of her tanks, her number painted on her buffer beam in GWR fashion and has not yet acquired her BR smokebox number plate.

A through train from Pontypool Road to Neath pauses at Hirwaun. The locomotive is ex-GWR 5700 Pannier Tank No 4688, which is having her water tanks replenished from the column on the platform. This was a member of the largest class of locos the GWR ever produced, with a total of 863 being built between 1929 and 1950. They were used on all kinds of passenger and goods duties across the former GWR network, and many were based in south Wales. No 4688 was built at Swindon in 1944 and withdrawn by BR in 1963.

The line had begun with the stiff climb from Pontypool Road up to Crumlin, and now at the other end there was an equally severe incline to take it down to Neath. Brunel's faith in the power of the larger locomotives that his broad gauge allowed encouraged him to propose a line which had four miles of gradients at 1 in 50 between Glyn Neath and the summit, which was near Hirwaun Pond. This was just beyond Rhigos Halt, opened in 1911 to serve a nearby pit. Goods trains heading down the incline had to stop here to allow the wagon brakes to be pinned down by the Guard. In 1960, a passenger train from Neath to Quakers Yard arrives at Rhigos Halt, hauled by ex-GWR 5600 class 0-6-2T No 6652.

Seen hard at work climbing the incline near Rhigos is a train from Neath to Pontypool Road, in charge of another of the ubiquitous ex-GWR 5600 0-6-2Ts No 5624.

In this 1961 view, both the train engine and the banking locomotive at the rear are working hard to lift a coal train bound for Aberdare up the bank. The leading engine is ex-GWR 5600 class 0-6-2T No 6695. This is one of the nine members of this class which have been preserved.

GLYN NEATH

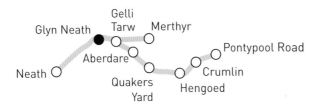

Glyn Neath · Gelli Tarw · Merthyr · Pontypool Road · Aberdare · Crumlin · Neath · Quakers Yard · Hengoed

Approaching Glyn Neath station with plenty of steam to spare is 0-6-0 Pannier Tank No 9412, on a service from Aberdare to Neath. The 9400 class was the last development of that classic GWR design, the Pannier Tank. They were designed by the company's last Chief Mechanical Engineer, F W Hawksworth, and the first ten were built at Swindon in 1947. A further 200 were ordered by BR from outside contractors, the last of these being delivered in 1956. With many of the duties for which they were earmarked being taken over by diesels, these engines had very short lives. No 9412 was built by Robert Stephenson & Hawthorns in 1950 and only lasted until 1963.

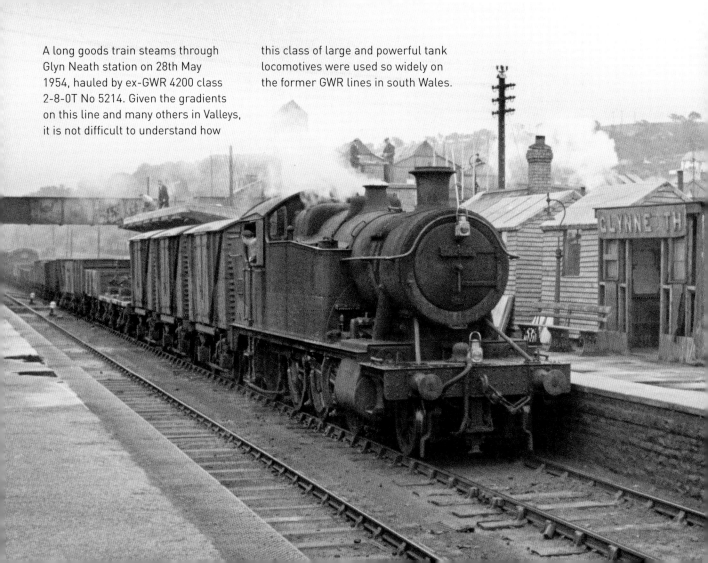

A long goods train steams through Glyn Neath station on 28th May 1954, hauled by ex-GWR 4200 class 2-8-0T No 5214. Given the gradients on this line and many others in Valleys, it is not difficult to understand how this class of large and powerful tank locomotives were used so widely on the former GWR lines in south Wales.

There was a small single road engine shed at Glyn Neath, whose purpose was primarily to supply engines to bank trains up the incline. On 12th May 1956, a pair of ex-GWR tank engines await their next banking duties at the shed. The locomotive standing by the large water tank at the entrance to the shed is 4200 class 2-8-0T No 4252.

With the hill climbing behind it, the line followed the broad, flat valley of the River Neath on its way to the coast. This view was taken near Resolven station, which was about three miles south west of Glyn Neath. A train from Neath to Pontpool Road is in charge of ex-GWR 4300 class 2-6-0 No 6361.

The GWR opened two halts on this part of the line in 1905, Melyncourt Halt and Clyne Halt, seen here. The very basic facilities provided included standard GWR 'pagoda' style corrugated iron waiting shelters on both platforms. What is also noticeable is the larger than normal space between the tracks, a legacy of the line's broad gauge origins.

NEATH

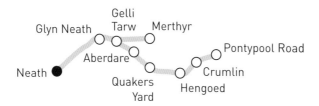

Glyn Neath   Gelli Tarw   Merthyr

Aberdare

Neath   Quakers Yard   Hengoed   Crumlin   Pontypool Road

When the line opened, VoN trains arriving at Neath used the South Wales Railway's main line station, where they reversed to run on to Swansea. Then, in 1863, the Swansea & Neath Railway opened with stations at Neath Low Level or Riverside as it was known from 1926 and Neath Abbey. This gave VoN trains direct access to Swansea without having to use the SWR station and tracks. The S&N route lost its passenger services in 1936 and now trains on the line to Pontypool Road again used the main line station, reversing there if they were running through to Swansea. Neath Riverside continued to be used by trains on the former Neath & Brecon line until that closed in 1962, along with all other passenger services to Brecon.

(See Lost Lines of Wales, Brecon to Newport). The South Wales main line crossed the tracks on an over bridge at the end of the platforms at Neath Riverside. This interesting view taken on 27th March 1948 shows a goods train on the main line, hauled by ex-GWR 2-8-0 No 4806. There was a serious coal shortage in Britain in 1947, and this led to 20 of the ex-GWR 2-8-0s being converted to burn oil. The oil tank on the tender of the locomotive, in place of the usual heap of coal, can be seen here. Those converted were re-numbered in the 4800 series. They had all reverted back to burning coal by 1950, when they also regained their original numbers. In this instance, No 4806 became again No 2832.

A view of Neath General in the 1970s looking towards Swansea. The connection to the line to Pontypool Road had been at the end of the platform, to the right of the picture, just beyond the building with the white gable. A signal box had also been located there, which controlled the junction and the now lifted track between the two running lines, enabling locos off the VoN services to run round their trains to proceed to Swansea.

CREDITS

Lost Lines of Wales – Vale of Neath
Published in Great Britain in 2017
by Graffeg Limited

Written by Tom Ferris copyright © 2017.
Designed and produced by Graffeg
Limited copyright © 2017

Graffeg Limited, 24 Stradey Park
Business Centre, Mwrwg Road,
Llangennech, Llanelli, Carmarthenshire
SA14 8YP Wales UK Tel 01554 824000
www.graffeg.com

Tom Ferris is hereby identified as the
author of this work in accordance with
section 77 of the Copyrights, Designs and
Patents Act 1988.

A CIP Catalogue record for this book is
available from the British Library.

ISBN 9781912050666

1 2 3 4 5 6 7 8 9

Photo credits

© Kidderminster Railway Museum: pages
12, 15, 16, 17, 22, 23, 24, 27, 28, 33, 35, 36,
37, 38, 45, 51, 52, 53, 55, 56, 57, 58, 59.
© W Potter, Online Transport Archive:
page 18.
© Blake Patterson, Online Transport
Archive: pages 21, 50.
© Martin Jenkins, Online Transport
Archive: page 30.
© W. A. Camwell/SLS Collection: pages
40, 42, 46, 48, 49, 61.
© R. F. Roberts/SLS Collection: page 63.